A BALL AND
A DREAM

TAMICA SMITH JONES, PHD

ME
WE
PUBLISHING

Scripture references are taken from the King James Version, New
International Version and other versions of the Holy Bible.
Pronouns for referring to the Father, Son and Holy Spirit are
capitalized intentionally and the words satan and devil are never
capitalized.

Publisher:
More Excellent Way Enterprises
www.mewellc.com

Second Edition
ISBN: 978-0-9864235-9-8

Library of Congress Control Number: 2017901090

Printed in the United States of America.

To my loves, T'Micah and T'Miyah, you are the surest reasons why I thrive in life; you are the holder of my legacy. You have brought me so much joy since your birth. T'Micah, I remember your first word being "hallelujah" – and we marveled. T'Miyah, you have kept me conscious of work life balance. I thank the Lord for the sweet transition into motherhood. I promise to guide you both with love in the way you should go.

To my parents who raised me in a stable, Christian, fun-loving environment. I am forever grateful for the opportunities that you gave me through ministry to serve and spread my wings.

To my loving siblings, aunts, uncles, cousins, nieces, nephews and church family, thank you for allowing me to be me. I appreciate the encouragement and love you have shown over the years.

To my grandmother, the Late Lee Ether Williams, thank you for the rich spirit you have poured into my life. Following your commitment, I will "trust in the Lord with all of my heart and lean not on my understanding, in all my ways I will acknowledge Him and I know that He will direct my path."

TABLE OF CONTENTS

FOREWORD

A Ball and a Dream gives us the feeling we are embarking on an adventure, both attention-grabbing and honest. She opens the door into a powerful journey of beginnings and endings where hope never dies. Dr. Smith Jones shares a secret formula to help us fulfill our dreams with strategy, faith, and a commitment to hard work.

She encourages us to maximize our gifts and talents while we are still young. The early years of focus and commitment propelled her into the life purpose unveiled in *A Ball and a Dream*. She courageously opens her heart to expose her less than perfect, but absolutely promising childhood. It is an incredible story that shows how you can merge two different worlds as described in her blended family and use the best from both. I love how she emphasizes love regardless of imperfections. Her perspective that dysfunctional living is the norm for human beings will enlighten and encourage you.

Even the Word of God includes one dysfunctional family after another. Remember marital rivalries within the family of Jacob and the sibling jealousies that led brothers to unite in a conspiracy against their father's favorite son? Yet, God used human dysfunction as the seed of His redemptive purpose.

Tattered lives such as these are our examples of how God works through imperfect beings to produce amazing results. I appreciate how she shares her excitement about becoming a blended family. In the midst of dysfunction, she discovered the vision for *A Ball and A Dream*. For her, it was just a new competition to win. She did win because she took the best from her experiences without losing her identity. She loved her one sister, mother and aunt, but still had plenty of love for a new dad, a big sister, and two brothers. What a delightful story of inclusiveness!

Dr. Smith Jones also magnifies the value of having a mentor. Many people view a mentor as someone available to spend time together, but she shows how we can learn from a distance by studying great men and women, using them as an inspiration for tenacity and technique. She describes using the example set by Michael Jordan in this way. She also shares the powerful influence that her dad and many wonderful coaches have had on her life.

It is remarkable to see how she accomplished each of the goals recorded for herself during her senior year of high school. Her frankness about the choices and consequences she made during her journey frees us to move forward in faith and not in fear.

Through the life of Dr. Smith Jones, God shows He is the God of another chance. This book is a must read for anyone who is struggling to focus, fulfill their vision and who is need of inspiration to keep going through every obstacle until the dream becomes today's reality. Through this inspiring book, Dr. Smith Jones challenges us with one word: DREAM!

She portrays a very exciting story of her life's journey toward the amazing success she enjoys today. I am encouraged how she explains confidently that vision and hard work will bring desired success.

A Ball and A Dream helps us to remember to start where we are, use what we have, and do what we can.

Archbishop Ruth W. Smith

INTRODUCTION

During the transition periods of my life, I would not have stayed focused without the support of so many important people and without the help of God Almighty, who is the leader of my life, the center of my joy and the reason I live full of peace, hope and prosperity. I thank Him for using me as a servant to share with the world *"the way, the truth, and the life."*

This book is dedicated to the millions of youths and young adults growing up in the backyards, streets and culs-de-sac playing ball. It is for those who are motivated by the thought of having a good, healthy and productive life through sports.

In the following pages, you will find the tools to successfully accept who you are, do what is necessary to attain your goals and make the right choices – the ones that will turn your dreams into reality.

Practical strategies for success will be identified, such as:

1. Pull away from the past and push toward your future

2. Use healthy relationships and support systems as key resources

3. Recognize passion and persistence as transferable characteristics

4. Expect results from your hard work and effort

5. Maintain a positive attitude and outlook on life

6. Create opportunity through goal-setting and determination

7. Gain experience through strong commitments and by investing in yourself

8. Identify your options in times of transition

9. Act in truth to yourself and to your values

10. Have fun in life and enjoy what you do

This book will encourage you to become a student of life by embracing changes, pursuing challenges and evaluating choices. It is a testimony of how you can succeed in spite of where you are from and what others say about you, even when obstacles are purposely put in your way. You will recognize the art of teaching, motivating and supporting others by sharing your story. Ultimately, this book is about the commitment to *your* game plan and *your* "next bold move" in life.

Tamica Smith Jones, PhD

CHAPTER 1

BORN A LEGACY

I was born Tamica Nakia Jones in Atlanta, Georgia on June 8, 1975. I do not remember much about my birth, so I had to have my mother, Ruth W. Smith, tell me this part of the story. My mom went to the hospital with labor pains on Friday, June 6, and I was delivered two days later, shortly after midnight.

According to my mom, I was born a beautiful, bald-headed baby. She remembers when she first cradled me in her arms like it was just yesterday.

Momma always dressed me in pretty pastels and frills. I wore dresses until I was old enough to decide what I wanted to wear. As soon as I could pick out my own clothes, I ditched the dresses and went "straight jeans."

My parents loved me and did their best to raise me in a Christian environment in spite of the many challenges they faced. They brought me up to have strong morals and taught me the importance of being confident and considerate of others. The person I am today as an adult is a direct result of the values they instilled in me. As a child, I was obedient, well-disciplined and very easy to handle. I wasn't fussy, nor did I cause trouble, so I did not require a lot of attention.

My young auntie and my father, a construction worker, were my babysitters, while my mom worked in the corporate world. My dad used to stay home on rainy days, which come by very often in Georgia, and eventually he became a stay-at-home dad. Back then, it was not widely accepted for a man to stay home and take care of the children, but it was a job my dad embraced before it became popular. He was also the cook for the household – a great one at that! I must say my auntie and father took very good care of me during the day. "You never had a fall or got sick," my mom recalled with pride. I loved my babysitters just as much as they loved me.

I was always very talented and athletic, even as a child. I took ballet, gymnastics and karate, and one of my fondest memories as a child was winning Miss Gresham Park in Decatur, Georgia. I caught on quickly to every new sport or activity because I was smart and independent. I am told that I stopped using a baby bottle at seven months old, and was potty-trained by my first birthday. Perhaps this independence came from having my father and a young adult as my primary caregivers. But, perhaps, being so independent at such a young age would come at a price – as I was to find out later.

Like most children, I looked forward to the holidays. It is not hard to find pictures of me with Santa at Christmas and the Easter Bunny at Easter. I always had a party on my birthdays. The funny thing is that my auntie always thought I was her baby doll, and these were opportune occasions for her to put me on display!

I actually thought my auntie was my sister until my real sister, Takiyah, was born in 1979. Takiyah and I have always been very close. Her birth caused my parents to move into our first home near a well-known church community in Decatur.

Then came a terrible blow! I was five and Takiyah only one. My parents divorced, and the seven-year marriage was over.

My mom tried to explain the situation to me as calmly as she could. She said it was best that my father left and she tried to raise me and my sister in an atmosphere without strife. One important thing my mom did was to always make sure we understood the value of our bloodline, both on her side and our dad's – DNA defined us and made us who we were. She would take her time to explain how different we would have been if we had been fathered by anyone else. All this did not make much sense to me then. But as I grew older, I understood my roots better and gained a greater appreciation and respect for my father, which led to a healing in our relationship over the years. All the same in those early days, my father did maintain a relationship with us. He would pick us up on weekends and buy us clothes, shoes and toys. I am always amused when I remember all the trips he made to the package store to get us our favorite dill pickles.

My mom remained single for about two years. And then the prophetic voice spoke. One day in church I suddenly leaned over to her and said, "Momma, I know who you should marry."

I guess I was tired of the Piccadilly's Restaurant food and having to go to bed at 7:00 p.m. Or perhaps I just wanted my mom to have someone special for her, the same way she gave me someone so special – my sister.

Whatever the reason, she responded, "Marry! How can you talk to me about marriage!" But after a while she leaned over to ask, "Who should I marry?" She then left it at that. Little did she … he … we all … know.

CHAPTER 2

BLESSED BY A BLENDED FAMILY

I would be the first to agree there is no limitation to your success. Whether you are a product of a dysfunctional family, an unplanned pregnancy, an adoption, whether you are divorced, a widower, a single-parent, whatever your setbacks, only your mentality can hinder you from accomplishing your dream. Walt Disney once said, "All our dreams can come true, if we have the courage to pursue them." You have to believe in yourself and have faith in God, who is able to do immeasurably more than all we ask or imagine, according to His power that is at work within us.

I remember the following childhood conversation vividly because it often flashes in my mind. I was playing with a friend after Sunday school when I noticed his dad, a well-known preacher. I said to my friend, "I know your daddy."

As part of a childish game, he responded, "No, you don't!" His dad was on my mind because he had recently taken my mother out to dinner.

Several Sundays later, I spoke prophetically to my playmate, "Your Daddy is going to be my Daddy."

For some reason, that made him extremely mad and he began chasing me all around the church and I ran for my dear life. He denied the marriage would ever happen and insisted it would always be just him and his dad. Little did we know that this prophecy would come to pass and we would become not just playmates but part of a "blended family." As for me, I embraced the thought of having more people to love, more people to share with and more people to call family.

My dad always said that he did not really just marry my mother. He became my dad! That special relationship with a true father figure in my formative years helped me become the healthy person I am today. I thought I was doing well with my mom and sister (which included occasional interactions with my biological father), but when I became a part of this blended family, I truly began living. I was so blessed with this new father that I boldly declared, "If Momma ever decides to leave Daddy, I'm going with Daddy." Thank God they made the decision at the beginning of their marriage and a declaration to the family that they were going to stay together no matter what! That was the best decision for a whole lot of lives. Our two families instantly became one because our parents laid down the law that we were not a step-family: no step-brother or step-mother, no such thing was encouraged, not even by my brother who had chased me around the church.

Who would not take advantage of having a big extended family? We went on family vacations and traveled in a mobile home to cities like Milwaukee and Chicago, not forgetting the trip to Disney World in Florida.

There was another big advantage. As a family of

five children that automatically gave us the benefit of having our own teams in the backyard. Maybe this is where my sports life started, although my dad claims my competitive spirit came from growing up with two brothers. We played baseball, basketball, football, and even raced on foot and on bikes. I remember when my youngest brother, Jeremiah (just five at the time), was on second base in a backyard game of baseball and we told him to run "home," he ran to third base, past home plate and straight into the house. We had to go inside and get him. It was a hilarious moment, one of the many moments I would cherish in my new home.

At first, it was rough for me to find my place as the elder child suddenly thrust into the middle spot. So I would compete with my eldest brother in nearly everything, from eating competitions to seeing who could stay up the latest – difficult for someone with a bed-at-7pm routine. Whatever Jermaine would do, I would try to do better. Unfortunately, when it came to eating, I could not devour an entire chicken wing or steaks the way he did.

As part of this blended family, my sister and I really experienced food. My dad would take us to Brick House Pizza in Lithonia, and we would eat all we wanted, play video games and stay up till late. As we got older, we moved from pizza joints to the more elegant restaurants, like those up in Buckhead. When it was just my mother, sister and I, we would eat one Piccadilly plate and only the healthier choices. Yes, the three of us ate one plate and we were satisfied. This was not because we were poor. My mom budgeted and was extremely health-conscious, ensuring we did not overeat.

I also remember how my brothers, sisters and I would team up to get Daddy his birthday present each year. It was a very serious matter deliberating and debating which gift would meet the interest of the majority. My dad used to say he always got something that we children would have wanted. For instance, some of our first gifts to him were an Atari system and a basketball hoop. That basketball hoop proved to be the best investment ever made for my family. Not only did we enjoy it but all the community children would come to play basketball at our house too. We played from lunch through dinner. And since our house was by the school bus stop, breakfast was often thrown in. We would always try to get a game in before school started.

After school, some of the children would not even go home. Their parents knew they were at the Smith's house. Our playmates had it made because we would invite them everywhere with us: dinner, church and even vacations when our respective parents agreed. What a blessing to grow up with not only brothers and sisters in my blended family, but also several friends who were connected to us like family! As one unknown author wrote, "Family isn't always blood. It's the people in your life who want you in theirs. The ones who accept you for who you are. The ones who would do anything to see you smile, and who love you no matter what."

CHAPTER 3

BOUND TO
BE A
BALLER

I started playing sports at home. My backyard, the genesis of it all, was a big grass field. In the driveway we had a full basketball court. My grandfather bought me my first basketball in the town of Greensboro, Alabama. Until it wore out, I carried that ball around everywhere. Although I played on mini, semi-organized teams as a young child, I most remember my time in middle school and high school athletics. It was in my backyard that I became a star in my own right. I carried my balling experience to the junior varsity (JV) team. I was a standout JV player and soon earned a spot to play for the varsity team because of my skill level. My dedication to the game and my skills acquisition was developed by my dad and the Michael Jordan "Come Fly with Me" video. Yes, my favorite player as a child, along with most children at that time was Michael Jordan. I never missed a Bulls game. My fanaticism for sports really derived from my obsession #23, better known as "MJ."

I started wearing the #14 jersey when I began

playing school basketball because I did not know any better, but when I was marked as a good player, I had to have the #23 jersey.

In the beginning, my dad said that I was the least skilled of all the ballers in the community, which consisted of all boys, some men, and three girls, including myself. When my playmates were gone and I thought balling for the day was over, my dad called me out for a game of 21 Points. He would take this opportunity to teach me how to dribble and shoot! I remember him placing chairs in the driveway, eight feet apart in a row. He would have me dribble up and down the driveway, and I had to do this without looking at the ball, weaving through the chairs, using both my left and right hand. My height was a disadvantage to me, even on my own court, because I was playing with taller boys and taller men. My dad started drilling me on the three-point shot, and this became one of his best investments to my game. Throughout my high school career, I led the Metro-Atlanta area on three-point shooting; that three-point shot became the catalyst for full basketball scholarships to colleges and universities all over the world.

My coaches were without a doubt good instructors too, allowing me to develop my natural skill. However, as I moved to the intercollegiate level, I focused more on fundamentals, because everyone was just as good as me. I remember the games where I put up the highest stats with dozens of points, several steals, and a few rebounds. I also remember the yells that came from behind the bench by my mother to the coach, "Take her out of the game, she has a bad attitude!" Yeah, I thought I was "all that" on the court, because most of the time I was the best player out there. Nevertheless, I had to humble myself at the next level; again, everyone played just as good as me.

I cannot forget my neighbors, mostly boys and some men, who would pick me to be on their teams. I cannot remember not ever getting picked for a team.

Perhaps, it was because of the risk of them being put out of my yard. Remember, I was the only one with a full basketball court near the bus stop for school. I remember the fights that occurred after losing. The frustration invaded the desire to win that was rooted deep in my heart. Sometimes, I would win the game but lose the fistfights, still knowing they would return tomorrow wanting to play. Suffice it to say, my character was being shaped through years of backyard playtime with family and friends – both good and bad.

Although my secondary school years came with a lot of disciplinary problems (talking too much in class, bad attitude, stubbornness, etc.), my dad always said that I was one of those students who made the other students think that I was not studying but still managing to make good grades. I thank God for those coaches, teachers, administrators, and supporters who cared enough for me to stay on me, work with me, and keep me disciplined. They really helped me to believe in myself and they helped me to understand the importance of a strong support system.

I remember loving basketball so much in high school that I would skip class to go to the gym and play all day. I never saw it as an offense; instead, it was what I loved doing and I risked being disciplined for my actions. One day, the school called home saying that I was absent; my mom was waiting for my arrival home that day. I was technically at school, but I skipped class to play ball in the gym all day. The only thing that saved me was the odometer in my car that showed I had only driven a few miles since the oil change that was performed just the day before.

Although stubborn as a donkey, my dad would say I was also as gentle as a lamb. I had a tough exterior, but because of my relationship with God and the teachings I received from the Word, I understood the importance of love, patience and forgiveness. I remember both of my parents always correcting me in love. For the record, I would rather have my dad discipline me with the rod, because he was so meek. He would make me cry even when he sat me down to talk. He would tell his grandchildren when he disciplined them, "It hurts me just as much as it hurts you, but I love you too much not to discipline you." The best part about Dad's correction was that we knew he was going to take us out for a treat before Mom got home to discipline us or after he had to discipline us. This demonstration of love from my dad taught me how to walk in love and forgiveness – characteristics that are needed for long-lasting, healthy relationships. Since everyone will fall short of being perfect, it is important for us to show mercy as the Bible states, *"Blessed are the merciful: for they shall obtain mercy"* (Matthew 5:7).

Contrary to my dad, my mother's discipline would make me want to disappear because she used the rod and talked through the entire ordeal. Her saying was, "I do not care if you like me or not as a parent because of this correction, you will love me more as you mature." Both forms of discipline held true and made me the person I am today – a better individual that could be likened to a morally upright citizen.

I remember during my senior year in high school my mom told me to write down my goals for the next five years. Even though I was not sure of what I would and would not accomplish within the range of that five years, I followed her directions, acting on my hopes, dreams, and faith of what I wanted in my life.

You must recognize that obedience in the small things is critical. Although we may feel that some things are unimportant or insignificant, we must grasp the fact that all God is asking is for us to be obedient – even when we do not feel like it or do not understand the direction that He is taking us.

Deuteronomy 27:10 states, *"Thou shalt therefore obey the voice of the Lord thy God, and do His commandments and His statutes, which I command thee this day."* When we are obedient to God, we position ourselves for His blessings to flow in our lives.

Here are the goals that I listed as a high school senior:

1. Go to college on a full basketball scholarship
2. Graduate from college in four years
3. Get a good, professional job
4. Marry a Christian fellow with a professional job who loved his mother

Guess what? By the grace of God, I accomplished my goals. My dad used to say that he thanked God for my diligence, discipline, and good work ethic that propelled me through my academic career. Most of all, he was thankful that their early investments of time and money and their sacrifices as parents ultimately paid off in full athletic scholarships for my undergraduate and graduate degrees. Additionally, sports would support my professional career, which advanced me towards obtaining a certificate degree with a concentration in Business Administration.

CHAPTER 4

BACKYARD BALLING PAYS OFF

After winning county, state, and regional games and awards, I had to make a very important decision in my life, a decision that would determine the direction and steps ahead of me. Where would I go to college? I soon realized that I was unprepared for my next bold move because I was not sure of the requirements for college-bound student athletes. I just knew I was good – even one of the best in the area – at girls basketball. I knew I did not want to live at home, but I wanted to be close enough for my family to come see me play. I was recruited by almost every historically black college and university you could name, but their dorm life discouraged me.

Finally, an AAU coach recruiting a shooter for her university, one that was moving to Division 1, contacted me. But, because I was unfamiliar with the university, I found myself therefore not interested. Nevertheless, I patiently listened to her and gained great knowledge of what I needed to do to be eligible to compete at the intercollegiate level. The coach was helpful, advising me of things that were important to look for in a school, such as a good fit academically, athletically, and socially. She also gave me the information that would be mandatory in order to compete at the intercollegiate level at any division, like the appropriate SAT/ACT scores, registering with the NCAA clearinghouse, applying to universities, and other pertinent things that could have easily been overlooked.

After traveling all over the south searching for a good fit, I took the AAU coach up on her offer to visit. I thank God they were still interested in me, because they stopped calling after I basically told them that I was not interested. I also told them that I would call if anything changed. I had officially written them off, but after an HBCU visit in Alabama, I still was not sure where I wanted go to college. That was when my parents suggested giving the coach a call. I called the coach on a moment's notice, and her staff seemed as if they were waiting for my call. I told them, "I am leaving another school in the area and would like to just stop by." They insisted that I did. They treated my family and I like royalty; I felt like a superstar in their eyes upon arrival. They welcomed me with open arms, and the visit seemed as if it was preplanned. They even had my jersey number and name hanging on a locker. To make a long story short, I signed the first full athletic scholarship on campus in that school's Division I history, which also allowed me to achieve my goal of graduating from high school with a full basketball scholarship.

To me, backyard balling had paid off; I was ready to take my superstardom to the next level. Little did I know that I would no longer be a superstar, but rather part of a team where everyone was just as good as me – if not better. If I did not do what was asked of me, there was a teammate on the bench waiting to come get me off the court. I had to be disciplined because I had gotten away with being a one-man team for so long. My freshman year at college, I experienced coming off the bench for the first time in my career. With five minutes off the clock in the first half of each game, I would substitute for a senior. It did not matter that I was a better shooter and a far better defender, she was an upper classman, putting in her time at the university. I was frustrated and eventually expressed verbally, "She only plays a few minutes; why am I not the starter?" I think my comments gave her a little more playing time. However, I played my role and still averaged double figures. In retrospect, I was out of line because I was privileged to not have to pay for my education, traveling up and down the East Coast, playing Division 1 basketball at the collegiate level.

It is an undeniable fact that we sometimes focus on the wrong aspects of life, and we give irrelevant things more consideration than relevant ones. Instead of being grateful for the situation and opportunities that I was blessed with in my life, I found simple concerns to stress over. I must say that my coaches and I did not see eye-to-eye a lot of times, but they insured my development on and off the court throughout my two years at the university. I expressed great gratitude to my first college assistant coach, the one who recruited, directed, and, even in the midst of disappointments during my freshman and sophomore years, compelled me to make "my next bold move."

I remember that academics were fairly easy throughout my career. I never had problems maintaining my grades, although I did not push myself toward Magna Cum Laude. But I did find that it got difficult being on my own, having to make mature decisions with my parents being at least three or more hours away. I would hang out all night on Thursday with my friends, and then try to make it to class on Friday. I remember struggling with finding a church home, because my parents had laid that foundation for me; it had become part of my life. Not that I did not know Christ, but I did not have enough experiences with Him to really appreciate who and what my salvation meant. On Sunday, I knew I needed to be in church, but unfortunately, it did not happen unless I went home during those two years of my life. I associated with people who practiced immorality, but I had praying parents. I remember my mother would write me letters saying that she was thinking about me, praying for me, and she would send me devotional readings in Scripture. I kept them and one read, "Hello Tam. I have been praying for you and the coaches a lot... Love mama!"

I had never been so independent before, and it was a new experience for me. I saw myself in a changed environment – an environment that accepted and encouraged your free will. No one cared if I stayed out all night or did not go to class in the morning. At times, I failed to act with self-control, a characteristic that had been part of my high school athletic history. I had to gain enough inner strength to be disciplined. I was selfish and wanted to enjoy my freedom, but I did not have the ability to choose the right people to hang out with or know how to control my environment. I decided that I needed some structure and consistency in my life. My parents knew it all along, especially my mom who called early in the mornings and sometimes in the middle of the night to ensure I was in my dorm room. When I would answer, she would just say she was thinking about me. During this period of my life, I found that the Word of God is true, *"The Lord shall preserve thy going out and thy coming in from this time forth, and even for evermore"* (Psalms 121:8).

On the outside I looked fine, but inside I was not doing so well. I think I was homesick, or maybe the campus culture at that time was not a good fit. Outside of my team activities, I felt socially disconnected in some way. One day I lashed out at a student on campus who called me out by name in the cafeteria. Without thinking clearly, I slapped her and was on my way to being escorted to jail for assault. Upon arriving to my dorm room only minutes after the incident, a voicemail on my phone from campus security directed me to report to the precinct. Instead, I packed my room up and went home to tell my parents of my actions and that I would get another scholarship just like I got before.

By the Grace of God, the same AAU coach who had given me the first intercollegiate opportunity got in touch with another coach who offered me a tryout for a second chance. This transition in my life really gave me a personal account of the importance of relationships: parents, coaches, and family. This experience also gave me a higher regard for my actions. I was compelled to let this transition in my life become a testimony and a testament to the compassion of God; He is always seeking to turn our situations around. In an instant, I became part of the NOW generation (Next Opportunity Waiting…waiting on me to act in faith).

God promised us an abundant life, but the truth is that God never promised us a trouble free life. What He promised was never to leave nor forsake us in that trouble. The reason why our problems cloud our judgment sometimes, to a point where we feel God is no longer with us, is because we fail to understand the reasons why we face certain circumstances.

Christians do not face trials and troubles as a form of punishment like sinners, but we face them because there is "good" that will come as a result of what we have gone through – sometimes we gain patience, compassion, and even a clearer understanding of our purpose. Jesus said, *"I have told you these things, so that in me you may have peace. In this world you will have trouble. But take heart! I have overcome the world"* (John 16:33). Like the process of refining gold, our lives, at times, must go through a tedious process, one that brings a "good" result in the end.

CHAPTER 5

HE IS A GOD OF A 2ND CHANCE

Although it seemed as if I was single-handedly destroying my own dreams one at a time, God still had a plan for me, one that made even the bad situations work for my own good. I truly believe the Word of God and I can be confident that the good work God started in me will be made complete and perfect until His return (See Philippians 1:6).

I remember being in the midst of my situation and getting a call from a coach concerning a tryout. My college assistant coach who had recruited me to my first scholarship was still behind the scenes making every effort to see me successfully complete my degree and compete at the intercollegiate level. She had called a coach at another college on my behalf and talked me up first class. She didn't even tell me of her solicitations, so, unexpectedly, I got a call from a Historically Black College and University (HBCU) coach to attend a tryout. It was an opportunity that I could not resist, but being immature, my first thought was the timing of the tryout was bad because I was already planning to go to spring break in Daytona Beach. But my "mama didn't raise no fool." I knew what I had to do. I guess Alabama was a part of my destiny because my family roots are there, and I got my first and second chances to play intercollegiate basketball in that state.

After answering the call, I went to visit the campus and tryout. I remember the coach telling me, "You are a shooter." And just like that I had a job. Ever since, I remember how my second college head coach brought out the passion in me. He would say at halftime after I had shot the ball at least fifteen times already, "You are my shooter, so don't stop shooting the ball." On a dismal shooting night, he would tell me, "You won't score a basket unless you shoot the ball." He made me one of the top players in the conference because he filled me with confidence. Starting anew for me was valuable because it built me up at a time when I was going downhill.

One of the most extraordinary things that

happened upon my transfer was that all of my credit hours were accepted by the new university. Therefore, I remained on track for graduation in four years, exactly as I set out to do in the personal goals I set in high school. I went on to have yet another successful athletic career and lead my team in scoring in all conference nominations.

This time I was determined to be a leader and not to fall into the same ditches that I had before. I had to walk in the truth of Deuteronomy 28:13, which states, *"And the Lord shall make thee the head, and not the tail; and thou shalt be above only, and thou shalt not be beneath; if that thou hearken unto the commandments of the Lord thy God, which I command thee this day, to observe and to do them."*

Ultimately, I used my experiences as learning opportunities, and I graduated with a Bachelor's Degree in Business. I know many people think that I should have been making more mature decisions at this stage in my life, but I did make at least one decision that would change things for me. My father was an Omega Psi Phi fraternity brother, and my college basketball coach was an Omega also. I thought it would be no problem pledging a Greek organization, one that I have always known would be the sorority for me.

It was during the final game of the season when the Delta chapter of Delta Sigma Theta was having its rush for the spring of 1997, and I had to be there. I made an attempt to pledge the year before, but because of my transferring status, I did not have the residency established that was required. Now in my senior year and only a semester away from completing my degree, I had to make a decision to pledge now or in graduate school. I wasn't even considering graduate school at the time, let alone pledging during basketball season because of my coach's rule against it. I remember my coach saying when I arrived, "My players do not pledge." But this was something that I had aspired to do since my matriculation into college. What should I do?

I knew it would cost me something, but I did not know it would cost me my full athletic scholarship. Yes, I decided to go for something that I thought I could not do without.

Well, I did it. I got my Greek letters, was given the line name of "Pippi" because of my long ponytails, and was number 47 out of my 65 line sisters. But what would I do concerning the cost of my final semester of college to obtain my degree? Yes, I only had one semester left, but my coach called me in and said how disappointed he was in my decision to pledge despite the team rules. Regretfully, he was not renewing my scholarship. I begged for sympathy, but he stood his ground for the sake of his leadership role, a decision I would one day come to understand.

I had one semester to graduate and no scholarship. What did I do? You got it - I got a job. I was working at a Footlocker shoe store during the summer months just to have a few extra bucks to take back to school with me. As it turned out, this job would give me more than money. During the summer before I graduated, a new manager joined the store. It happened to coincide with the week of my birthday, and I invited all of my co-workers to a house party, one that I was known to have when my parents were out of town. Everyone was there, including a few celebrities from the "ATL" like Lisa "Left Eye" Lopez (RIP). We would party until the break of dawn.

The new manager came too. He said he got a special invitation and came to the party with his work clothes on. Upon his arrival, we got to talking about our interests, especially sports. We even discussed the first university I went to out of high school; he also had a basketball scholarship offer to attend.

After that, we went back to work at Footlocker and became great friends. I even started giving him my sales and, in exchange, he would buy me lunch. I don't think he bought me lunch because I gave him sales though. It was probably more because I was bringing him my grandmother's breakfast and his favorite dish of hamburger steak, gravy, and rice on occasion. Nevertheless, it ignited our hearts for what would become a marriage three years later.

The summer was coming to an end and I had to return to school for my last semester, but I still had no way to pay for it. I could not bring myself to ask my parents who had been so supportive over the years, encouraging me in spite of my circumstances. They had planned financially for other things since I was going to school on a scholarship. So, I knew I had to figure out this one on my own. I went to the new cross country coach on campus and asked if I could please run for the fall semester on a scholarship. I told her the situation and encouraged her to speak with my basketball coach, who I knew would vouch for my being a pure athlete and give her other great attributes. I also knew my basketball coach just had to set an example with me on the basketball team, and I respected his decision. Sure enough, she spoke to him, and he gave me his blessings. I got the cross country job, but that meant I had to run three miles a day, which I did not like at all. After the second or third cross country meet, I gave up the running for an assistant coaching job. I asked the coach if she could please let me be an assistant because I would die if I ran another mile or another trail in the rain. She concurred and allowed me to do all of her administrative work, something I happily accepted.

I began to appreciate all of the "volandatory" (a hybrid of "voluntary" and "mandatory") services provided in administration at my church when I returned home from college. All of the computer typing, data entry, filing, answering the switchboard, and other tasks required by the church office administration proved to be transferable skills as a student assistant to my coach. Those experiences were priceless, and my determination to do whatever it took to graduate in four years gave me the confidence to "find a way or make one." I was more interested in results than in excuses, which is why I encourage others to volunteer their time and give back to the community - that faithfulness will be honored and those planted seeds will be fruitful in due season. 1 Peter 2:21 declares, *"For even hereunto were ye called: because Christ also suffered for us, leaving us an example, that ye should follow his steps."* Peter encourages us to get involved in the lives of others, but not because we are paid to do so; instead, it should happen as a result of our relationship with Christ, who so freely served us.

Although I was essentially dismissed from one university and my scholarship was decisively revoked at another, I was still able to make good on my second goal of graduating from college in four years (and one semester). You must believe that you can overcome any situation or circumstance.

When you fall, never stay down. Get back up, and go in a different direction. It is also important that although stressed, distressed, and sometimes depressed, you acknowledge that, "*Greater is he that is in you, than he that is in the world*" (1 John 4:4). In the midst of what looked like an obstacle, my first opportunity in coaching administration was manifested, and it was a life-changing moment.

CHAPTER 6

DETERMINATION
BIRTHS
OPPORTUNITY

I truly believe that God gave me a second opportunity because of the determination that has been in me since birth. He knew that if given the opportunity, I would move forward in His purpose for my life of sharing His good news through sports and the athletic profession. I am a living testament of the fact that *"the Lord is good to those whose hope is in him, to the one who seeks him"* (Lamentations 3:25). Early in my life I wanted to be a lawyer. Perhaps, I would have pursued that career if it were not for the opportunity that opened up to me just as I was graduating with my Bachelor's degree. I thank God that I never had to go looking for my next move. He always opened alluring doors of opportunity for me. I did not have to strive or toil to manufacture opportunities for myself. It was not by my might, but by His grace and great power. I know very well how easy it is to try to control every last detail of your life. Of course it is good to have a mission in life, but it's important to step back and think about whose desires you are seeking. Philippians 2:3 states, *"Let nothing be done through strife or vainglory; but in lowliness of mind let each esteem other better than themselves."* I have learned not to allow pride to be my guide, but the Holy Spirit. He is my guide and my counselor. When I follow His leading, God's kingdom is established on Earth and I am able to rest in His peace, knowing that in all things, God works for the good of those who love Him, who have been called according to His purpose (See Romans 8:28). This is why I am more determined to stay in the will of God more than anything else because in His will is where we are made perfect.

I have promised that each day of my life I would be the best I could be for God, myself, and for others. I realize that this commitment is not just for my self-gratification, but for those who need me as an example to model their dreams and ultimately to glorify God. There is no doubt opportunity will come, but will you be ready, brave enough, humble, and obedient enough to receive it and give God the glory?

I was 21 years old and planning for graduation from Alabama A&M University in Huntsville, Alabama. I had not quite decided what I would do with a Bachelor's Degree in Business Management, but always had the opportunity to work for my parents in the ministry. Of course, I reflected occasionally on being an entrepreneur, but had no clue of what I would pursue. One thing that I was certain of was that, regardless of whatever wishes or dreams I had, ultimately, God's will would prevail. He has sworn, *"Surely, as I have planned, so it will be, and as I have purposed, so it will happen"* (Isaiah 14:24).

Just as I needed an answer, God showed up! I thank my assistant collegiate basketball coach for thinking of me when he was given an opportunity as a head coach. He phoned and offered me a graduate assistant basketball and volleyball position, and, without thought, I took it the day after obtaining my bachelor's degree. The deal was to pay for my graduate studies, provide me with housing, and make available other perks that would come with the position, like traveling per diem, networking, etc. I thought this would be a great move for me and surely it worked in my favor. I knew that it was important for me to be obedient and I felt that the Holy Spirit was guiding me. Therefore, peace ruled my heart.

Coach said, "I always knew that you had potential by your charismatic character." That is what had convinced him the most to call me for the position. He made the call and I answered. Before I knew it, I was wearing polo coaching shirts, planning travel, scouting athletes, and strategizing game plans. When I look back at how God worked everything out in my life, I cannot help but just be in awe. Surely, when God shows up, He shows out, so that only He gets the glory. I could not and I would not even dare take credit for what He has done in my life. No one can craft a plan and make it come to fruition like the Master Himself. It was His craftsmanship that created my career of coaching and a game plan for my life. It was fun, but it also meant that

I had to get back in the classroom as a graduate student, and that was horrific.

My first day of class, I met a friend who had gotten his undergraduate degree from the university. He was familiar with the environment and had classmates who had graduated from the Public Administration program. He was trying to hook up with me, and, of course, I was smart enough to befriend him. We turned out to be really close and partnered in our coursework, studying sessions, projects, and even graduated together. He was surely a person that I needed, like a guardian angel during those times when days got tough, coursework was challenging, and expectations were high. He was a shoulder to lean on and a great source of support. Many people out there do not have anyone at all, but I was grateful to have him in my life. I remember calling home after my first "F" on a test, telling my parents that I wanted to come home. They asked, "Why?" I replied, "I didn't need to do this because I had a degree and needed to get a real job."

My mom emphatically expressed, "You have a real job, and that is to go to graduate school to become the best graduate assistant coach you can be."

After her statements, she didn't even say, "Hold on. Here is your dad." She just gave him the phone.

My dad got on the phone and asked, "What do you need to get a job for?"

"I don't have any money," I replied. I was broke and living off a meal plan wasn't fun as an adult. Don't get me wrong, I was thankful for the little I had because it was more than what others had, but I could not ignore my less than ideal situation; the struggle was definitely real. I had a car but couldn't drive it without gas. Remember, I was getting my school paid for and housing, but no financial stipend for spending. I would save my per diem from games to make it through the week.

My dad said conclusively, "How much money

do you need?" You wouldn't believe the reply I gave, "$100 a month." Now you know that I wasn't ready for the real world. My dad immediately put $200 in my account, and I think I made it with that the rest of the semester. Occasionally, my parents would come down, and we would go to Sam's Club Warehouse and buy food for the semester. They would feed me a good meal, leave me with money, and hit the road back home all in two or three hours. Through my parents, God certainly supplied my needs; He was and still is my Jehovah Jireh, my provider.

Unfortunately, the coach who hired me was not going to be returning the following year to coach, and I was given the opportunity to be the interim head coach of two sports, volleyball and basketball. This opportunity was offered only because I was determined I could handle the responsibility successfully, until a permanent candidate was hired. As the interim head coach, I was responsible for the entire operations from scholarship allotment to equipment, travel, and game strategy. I had a successful term by taking both programs to their conference tournament. In basketball, we had a winning season (the first in five years), made it to the semi-finals, but lost to the champions. However, maintaining a good retention rate was my pride and joy, because it helped us build the program and illustrated the seriousness of my academic focus. I was certain that I would take the opportunity to coach and make the best of it.

As a youngster in the profession, I had a lot of critics, a lot of experienced coaches who thought they could do the job better than me and others who wondered why the university would give a 22-year-old such a big task. I thank God for the President of the University, for whom I gained a great deal of respect. He always showed up for our home games and gave me a nugget of encouragement each time we crossed paths. I could not have made such a challenging transition without the help of the men's basketball coach, who had the experience and knowledge that I needed to progressively lead my team. I spent a lot of time studying, preparing, and inquiring about the sports to ensure the best possible outcome. I knew I was a leader and that I could motivate the girls I coached to work hard in the classroom in order to make it to the court. I was not so naïve to think I had all the answers. My ultimate goal was to see my student-athletes graduate and get the same opportunity that I had in life upon obtaining a degree. It was important, as I took control of this team, that I did what I did well and enjoyed it, because that was my indication that God's plan was gradually being confirmed in my life. This period brought great fulfillment and hope to my life.

I would have loved staying at the university, but I was in the position on an interim basis. As a candidate for graduation with my master's degree, a college from my hometown calls me for duty. I thank them for the opportunity that solidified my leadership skills. The memories and relationships that were built over the years are indelible.

CHAPTER 7

OPPORTUNITY BUILDS LEADERSHIP

You must know that if you never take a chance, then you will never increase your opportunities. I realized that coaching at such a young age was a risk, but it was also a great opportunity. Actually, it became an act of faith in full confidence in God's Word that I am more than a conqueror through Him that loved me (See Romans 8:37). I had to humble myself and submit to building trust, confidence, and respect with young adults very close to my own age. It filled me with a consciousness of accountability, because I had to walk upright in an effort to embrace their attention.

Being a coach, I also needed to walk in wisdom, courage, and relentless faith in order to deal with and inspire the young adults that were under my leadership; with time, I would come to realize that faith was the one thing I needed the most. I realize now more than ever that the success I achieved was based not only on my leadership skills, but also on my willingness to trust God and His purpose for my life, though sometimes I had to let go of my will and allow my God to move.

Taking the chance to begin a future in sports administration, which was natural in my life, was a good move in developing my leadership skills. But how do you know which opportunities you should take? I would advise, based on my experiences, that if something opens up for you and if it is a progressive move, taking the opportunity is the right decision. Only when you take advantage of these opportunities will you truly strengthen your leadership abilities. You can't be afraid of opportunities, but I would also cautiously make every effort to stay in God's perfect will. Throughout my life, I have learned that there are two wills of God: His permissive will and His perfect will. I think that with permissive will, He allows us to make choices that are based on our own command. These choices and experiences could prove to turn out bad, but God allows it, I think, because this opens the doors of opportunity. Even if things look like they are not going well, I like to say, "It is working for my good" (See Romans 8:28). He has given us the gift of free will and because He is a merciful and gracious God, even when we take the wrong turn, He is always there to guard us in all our ways. Like I mentioned earlier, God does not break His promises. No matter what kind of situation you may find yourself in, take comfort in the fact that, *"The Lord himself goes before you and will be with you; he will never leave you nor forsake you. Do not be afraid; do not be discouraged"* (Deuteronomy 31:8).

The call from a college in Atlanta asking me to bring my talents back to my hometown was a great day in my life. I was not anticipating it, because I had been away from home for six years attending college (four years obtaining my Bachelor's Degree in Business Management and then two more working toward my Master's Degree in Public Administration). I would have never expected my cousin, who is coaching at this college along with my uncle, to call, saying, "Hey, the athletic director wants to know if you are interested in coaching the women's volleyball and basketball teams." I was excited and started preparing a resume right away.

This was a great opportunity, and while heading to the Super Bowl in Florida, I still managed to send my application via FedEx to the Director for his review.

I was called for an interview where they offered me the position of head volleyball coach/assistant women's basketball coach. Although I was more interested in basketball since it was my specialty, I was eager to broaden my perspective and enhance my gifts. I knew nothing concerning coaching the technical aspect of volleyball, but God was working with me – without me even being aware of it. I remembered that as part of our athletic family responsibilities in my undergraduate studies, we had to set up for the volleyball team, be in attendance at each home game, and even serve as line judges during competition. I had learned a lot during that time about the sport, but I didn't know that I would need the information at a later date.

Both success and opportunity will not come without challenges, but God gives you the tools and qualities that will prepare you when the opportunity does come. Sometimes you may wonder whether God really understands what you're up against, but trust me, He knows exactly what obstacles you are facing. He knows that you are not facing anything new under the sun. Not only that, He has equipped you with everything good for doing His will and all the tools to overcome anything that may be standing in your way (See Hebrews 13:21). Everything you put your mind to and hands to are transferable skills for your future endeavors.

I was honest in the interview about my experience, but they were more interested in my willingness to learn as much as possible and my ability to take the team on a new path. The transition back home for my first professional job was smoother than I anticipated. But even with wise decisions, such as living at home with my parents, came its own set of dynamics, issues that paled in comparison to being able to start work with stability.

I must interject here that, as a young adult, I appreciated that my parents offered me their home after being away at college for six years. They helped me to keep my goals in perspective, because they didn't offer me a bedroom but rather a futon in the sunroom – even though they had two empty bedrooms available. This arrangement established in my mind that it was not a place I would stay, but instead a launching pad for me to get started in life.

My parents could have allowed me to get an apartment, thus throwing away my $31,000 a year salary. Instead, they realized the benefit of providing an environment for me that had structure. No, I couldn't stay out all night, even though I tried it a time or two. I could not blast my radio or have company that was not decent or even allow males in my room. It was just like my former years at home, except I was older. These were the rules I have always had to abide by, and I have developed because of them. I had a place to lie my head,

I was able to eat what was cooked, and I made my own money to pay for expenses incurred on a daily basis.

My oldest sister had attended this institution where I would start my full time coaching and administrative career. Even more, my cousin and a mutual friend had played basketball and recently graduated together. It was indeed a homecoming to be given the opportunity to work on a campus I had grown up on as a child. My uncle had worked his way through the ranks as a coach and athletics director. I naturally felt at home, and my name was known upon my first step on campus. I remember getting visitors to my office asking to see the volleyball coach. When I replied, "I am she," they seemed flattered. Remember the guy that I spoke of earlier who came into Footlocker as a manager? We had kept in touch over the years, but we would only see each other when I came home from college to visit. Upon my acceptance of my new position in Atlanta, he began to put word out that I was coming and, as God would have it, he introduced me as his girl. As a well-respected man and a graduate of the institution himself, he caused others to celebrate my arrival and made it a high-spirited event for me.

My return home definitely gave us quality time together, but I never thought he would be my husband until one day my mother asked, "Who is the special guy friend in your life?" I didn't expect that question, but you know mothers have a special way of obtaining information. I figured it was time to move out, but I attempted to answer the question. At that time in my life, I had a few significant others. I thought I was just living and loving life. I would go out to eat with a friend, go see a movie with another – all in good fun. So I thought "special friend," and guess who I mentioned? Yeah, "the guy who came in as a manager at the Footlocker that summer before I got my undergraduate degree." Little did I know that statement would bring life to our relationship. I should have known better since it is no secret that the tongue has the power of life and death (See Proverbs 18:21). What we speak out of our mouths is more powerful than we realize.

I just knew out of all the guys that I was interacting with, he was the man who most closely matched my wish list – yes, the list I wrote in high school after a life lesson from my mom on goal setting. I wanted a husband who was at least on my level – or should I say - who was a Christian, someone who had a good professional job, who loved his mother and who had no children. The most important thing for me was to be someone who had a heart for God, just like myself, and was completely living for Jesus. I was sure that if I ever got into a relationship, I would not settle for anything less than a partnership rooted in the Word of God and centered in Christ. He had all of that going for him and, while some of the other guys were really good candidates, his 6'4, dark and handsome profile didn't hurt either. He had won me over.

Once I got settled into my role as full-time head coach, the program made a decision to move to Division I, which was the highest level of competition. The university's athletics program was competing at the Division II level, which is considered mid-level competition (Division III being the lower level and one that does not offer athletic scholarships). Consequently, along with the move, we had to create a tougher schedule. Every year I was able to bring in girls who worked hard in the classroom and on the court. We doubled our wins each season, I was able to retain the student-athletes at high numbers, and we seemed to have good camaraderie and chemistry. This was success to the team, department, and the college, something to really be proud of while transitioning to such a high level of competition. The opportunity to coach at this level fortified my vigor as a leader.

Within two years, I moved up in the athletics administration and was offered a senior woman administrator title. This designation and appointment by the NCAA is to involve female administrators in a meaningful way in the decision-making process in intercollegiate athletics. The appointment is intended to ensure representation of women's interests, experience, and perspective at the institutional, conference, and national levels. It is "the highest-ranking female administrator involved with the conduct of a member institution's intercollegiate athletics program" (NCAA Constitution 4.02.4).

I remember being called from the main office to meet with the Athletic Director. He asked if I would be interested in the appointment, which gave me an indication that the university was obviously interested in me filling it. Immediately this became another opportunity, something that would advance me to a higher leadership role. He went on to state that they wanted someone who had their master's degree and, at the time, I was one of only two females within the department with the degree. I said to myself, "Wow, my Master's of Public Administration degree is already paying off." By that time, I had no doubt about the doors of opportunity that God was leading me to and I had faith that what He opens, no one will shut (See Revelation 3:7). Soon thereafter, I replied with my interest in the new position.

This was an exciting administrative job and I had the opportunity to get significantly involved in more than just the coaching aspect of athletics, but also other sports program supervision, budget management, monitoring implementation of gender-equity plans, and I became an active member of professional athletic organizations. As I was in the position for just a year, major administrative adjustments within the department took place. Yet again I was in a position of favor to move up the ladder of administration into an assistant athletic director for women's sports as a new director was appointed. Once we made our Division 1 move and my expertise showed forth, I made a leap into the senior associate athletic director position, which truly gave me the opportunity to oversee the entire program. All of these opportunities in leadership prepared me tremendously for what was ahead in my career. I thank God there was no respect of persons in leadership at this institution. I especially appreciated the confidence the Director of Athletics had in my talents and gifts in administration. He was not intimidated and he did not withhold opportunity from me; instead, he eagerly guided my path to success in athletic administration.

I was feeling a bit emotional in the summer of 1999 and I mentioned to my significant other that I think he could be the person that I could spend eternity with. I didn't want him to take it as a pressing comment, and I told him it was only for his information. He could have taken it and then done what many men do – nothing. But being the mature and wise man that his parents raised, he proposed to marry me within a few months.

I remember we were at my parents' home playing pool, and he stopped and hugged me, saying, "I think I can spend the rest of my life with you." I thought he was playing, as we often did; we always had lots of fun together because we had become friends. I told him to call his mom and tell her if he was serious, because I knew the relationship they had. He picked up his cell phone, called immediately, and put me on the spot because she asked to speak to me. I found out he had been talking to her about me for a while; I didn't even know he was that serious.

That was not enough; I asked him to perform the ultimate act of sincerity. "If you're serious, go tell my dad." My dad is the bishop, and he wouldn't play with him. My boyfriend responded, "Go tell your dad I want to see him." I did. "Send him back," was my dad's reply. We went walking back, and I was walking as if we were going before the judge himself. My boyfriend though, he went courageously, shaking hands and hugging my parents. Then he said, "I would like to marry your daughter." My dad easily gave his blessing, "OK son. You will need to set up a meeting with the pastor." From that point, we went through marital counseling and started planning our wedding.

Within six months, he had purchased a house, because I refused to get married and move into an apartment. He expected this because I had lived with my parents and had my housing paid for throughout college. I didn't want to throw my money away, but rather I wanted to invest in our future. I had been to enough young women's conferences, heard numerous sermons and knew Proverbs 31 back to front, so I knew what it took to be a noble wife and I was determined to start married life strong. Within a year we were married. It started with a question from my mother that spoke life and led to a wedding in the same place where we got to know each other best, my parents' home. I must say I learned the importance of speaking life. Whatever you hope for, wish for, or want out of life, speak it, feed it, and it will come to pass.

Just when I thought that things were so good in my personal life and I was in a good place with my job, moving up the ladder of opportunity and on my way to happily ever after, the college went through its accreditation period. Hoping for the best possible outcome, re-accreditation, we got the worst results. I remained steadfast because I'm a firm believer in not moving unless God says so. I know that He put me in the ship at the institution for a reason, and that was to develop my athletic administrator career through relationship, stewardship, and fellowship, out of which would ultimately take me to the championship of life. Many jumped ship, others were cast out, and those of us who stayed on the sinking ship found out one day that our program was instantly discontinued. It was a sad day, and I had not planned for it because I was content and riding my course in life.

Suddenly I was jobless, taking trips to the unemployment office, and feeling uncertain about my future. Everyone kept in contact so that we could help each other out if we heard of any job availabilities. Many got jobs right away, some took jobs that weren't necessarily of their interest, and others, like me, waited for God to move on our behalf.

During this transition in my life, I found out that I was pregnant with my son. After three years of marriage, I began to feel the pressure of finding employment. I decided I would just take some time to do nothing. In the midst of this job uncertainty, here I was in the new experience of motherhood. I was convinced I was a bona fide adult now because I had been laid off from a job and I was expecting my first child. Thank God for the leadership skills perfected in me during my tenure because it directly fabricated great character, and little did I know that the true character test was about to come.

CHAPTER 8

LEADERSHIP BUILDS CHARACTER

Anytime you are in a leadership position, you must know that your character will be tested. Before taking up their roles as leaders, many great men and women of God in the Bible endured trials. Even Jesus' disciples said that we must go through many hardships to enter the kingdom of God. *"Confirming the souls of the disciples, and exhorting them to continue in the faith, and that we must through much tribulation enter into the kingdom of God"* (Acts 14:22). God calls us all to be part of His kingdom and I believe He chose me for a specific role. Although my character was tested, I was not mature enough to pass the test until I was thirty-years-old. I had to earn the right to call myself a leader. It was only then that I understood why many are called, but few are chosen (See Matthew 22:14). The control and power that comes with leadership may be pleasing, but it comes with a price that you must be ready to experience. I learned that God's call to leadership was not about honor, merit, and glory; it was about service and surrender. I must say that I was not ready for my character to be challenged in my next leadership position. One day, I ran into a coach at a university in Atlanta who had recruited me out of high school, but I had declined the offer because I didn't want to stay home for my undergraduate study. As a matter of fact, his employer and my former employer were rival schools. Every time we coached against one another, my team won. We became good associates. When I asked him about his situation, he gave me a hesitant response, "It's good; you just can't ruffle any feathers."

I didn't comprehend the depth of his reply, and I immediately thought it might be a good move to join his institution. I had never been in a dreadful job since entering the workforce, so I had no intention of ruffling feathers. I thought this would be a good opportunity, and I interviewed with the director and started working right away. This transition in my life was good for my maturation, strengthening my character, and propelling me forward to my "next bold move" in life. I was absolutely confident that no matter what lay ahead of me, God would go before me and make the crooked places straight (See Isaiah 45:2). I was able to acquire the same leadership title, but I was not given the same authority as I had in the position I formerly enjoyed.

This was a test of my character because I had to learn how to step back and operate in a role that was uncertain from day to day, that varied with emotions, and that essentially suppressed my ability to lead. My heart became weighed down with anxiety and the cares of life. Don't get me wrong, I know very well that we should not let our hearts be troubled, neither let them be afraid (See John 14:27), but at the time, I had not matured enough to fully cast my anxieties on the Lord. In my first year in my new leadership position, I noticed a bit of dissension within the department, but I tried to remain encouraged and help work through issues. I learned 2 Timothy 1:7 early in life, *"God hath not given us the spirit of fear; but of power, and of love, and of a sound mind."* I was confident that things would get better just with my being on the team.

But by my second year, it was clear that I had become a part of the problem despite my efforts to be part of the solution. Many within the department rallied around me because I worked hard to empower others. I was dignified in the way I spoke and my words were helpful for building others up according to their needs; I tried to benefit those who listened (See Ephesians 4:29). I thought this would earn me a good reputation amongst my colleagues, but I soon realized that was not the case at all. A few of us devoted a lot of energy to uniting the department, while others were intimidated and found pleasure in feeding the drama. One of the disciples, James, says that we are to *"Consider it pure joy, my brothers and sisters, whenever you face trials of many kinds, because you know that the testing of your faith produces perseverance"* (James 1:2-3), but this is easier said than done. It was hard to remain focused, but I found strength in my ability to trust in God, knowing that He was in control. Ultimately, I surrendered the situation to God. I let perseverance finish its work so that I would be mature and complete, not lacking anything (See James 1:4). I constantly thought to myself that in a healthy environment, no one feels threatened, but I knew that by maintaining the right perspective in life, I could withstand the fiery trials and temptations.

I cannot vividly remember ever wanting to quit anything in my life, but it had come to that point. I felt like my life was being shattered in such a tumultuous work environment. Like never before, I missed something after it was gone. I found myself reminiscing, comparing and contrasting, and wishing I was somewhere else. It was easy to remember times when I was happier and felt more fulfilled in my work. Don't mistake these feelings to mean that I wasn't in a good situation, because this institution was one I had admired over the years, and was definitely one that I have been blessed with and have benefited from as an employee and associate. I understood that the connectivity was part of the life of the organization, and they saw the value in it. Even though the opportunity at the institution gave me the public platform to work within my purpose, I got in a funk because I was being consumed with negative energy all around me. I pleaded with God that I would continue to grow and thrive despite all the odds being against me. Even with all of this going on, by God's grace, I seemed to be just fine both personally and professionally.

I won the Southern Intercollegiate Athletic Conference Volleyball Coach of the Year Award in just my second season at the university with a record of 27–11, the best volleyball record in school history and a vast improvement on the first season of 9–22. My student athletes were excelling in the classroom and on the court with the all-conference awards. God had sent me assistant coaches, who volunteered faithfully each season. I finished my advanced degree certificate program, graduated from the NCAA Women's Coaches Academy, and, most importantly, family life was good. But even with all of this success, I just wasn't feeling my best, and something in my life was going astray. I felt stagnant and sluggish like never before. I thought through the answer, but I didn't talk to anyone about it because I didn't know how. I was a wife, mother, sister, daughter, coach, mentor, and confidant, so I had to remain strong on the outside, but inside I was pathetic. As long as I focused on what was wrong with me, I got nowhere. Once I opened myself up to the possibilities of being in God's will, I knew I was going in the right direction. I knew that God was with me, but I didn't know what He was doing at that time. I took solace in the fact that the Lord has said, *"For I know the thoughts that I think toward you…thoughts of peace, and not of evil, to give you an expected end"* (Jeremiah 29:11). Despite how weak and weary I felt, I simply held on to the promise that God would instruct me and teach me in the way I should go. We must understand that there is a process for success; I was just going through my process.

One Wednesday, I felt so broken, disgusted, and fed up, to say the least, with what my situation had become. I had a home volleyball game and got into the office late because my son had an appointment with the doctor. Upon my arrival, I read an email from the university president that said we were getting raises, and that they would be based on our performance evaluations that occurred in June. I got a favorable appraisal and was content with the director's evaluation of my performance for the fiscal year. I thought nothing further of the review but hadn't received my copy for months. One day I found the back cover of my appraisal in the office copier, and I inquired about its position but I couldn't even get a candid response. Immediately I contacted the human resource office for a copy of my appraisal, and they gave me a copy of the year before. As you might imagine, now that we were up for raises, I was quite interested in my appraisal. Right away, I asked my graduate assistant to go to the human resource office to pick up a copy of my latest review. Upon receipt, I was shocked; my performance evaluation had been drastically changed from "meets requirements" to "does not meet."

I felt betrayed, angry, and definitely knew that I was in a place that I didn't belong. I had endured the hardships and believed that God could use my presence as a way to reach out to people and draw them to Christ. At that point, enough was enough. I had P.R.I.D.E. because I was going to be firm in my *professionalism*. Although I wanted to give a few people a piece of my mind, it was important that I kept a level head. I also stayed professional because my parents were out of the country at the time, and I didn't want them to return home with me in the news. What's more, I knew I had a family to feed and needed to act in a responsible manner regarding the circumstances. Don't think that it didn't cross my mind how inequitable the situation was, but my pride and character made me act *respectfully*. The words from Ephesians 4:26, *"Be ye angry, and sin not: let not the sun go down upon your wrath,"* rang in my head as I remembered all the sermons on anger that had been preached throughout my life. I was determined not to give the devil a foothold by acting hastily and potentially stirring up conflict. I slept on the incident, hoping by morning the anger would have dissipated. Unfortunately, when morning came, I was still very upset, but I gave my director a call.

I opened the conversation by asking, "Are you not satisfied with my performance on the job?"

Empathetically, I was told, "I don't have a problem with your performance. What are you talking about?"

I was upfront and said that I was looking at my altered performance evaluation. Basically, I fell short of getting anything resolved, other than hearing his response, "I understand the feeling of a poor performance evaluation. I received one also, and I am not getting a raise." What that had to do with me, I still failed to connect. I was under the impression that I had a good evaluation, which indicated in my initial review and signed off on as my final assessment. You know that for me this was a tough response and I hadn't always responded so serenely to an adverse situation. I knew I wasn't fighting with the person, but the *spirit* of the person, *"For our struggle is not against flesh and blood, but against the rulers, against the authorities, against the powers of this dark world and against the spiritual forces of evil in the heavenly realms"* (Ephesians 6:12). I knew I had to be the better person, but I must admit that I lost a lot of respect for the individual. However, I reached deep within to maintain my respect as unto the Lord.

I was not treated with *integrity* in the situation because altering my evaluation fallaciously was definitely unfair and unethical. I decided to follow the grievance process of the institution since they had always been reputable in their dealings. You know what they say is true: "Life is not fair." I considered it as defamation of my character because the alteration was erroneous and intended to impede my progress. The director didn't even have the audacity to make comments in the space provided regarding what areas I needed to improve on in an effort for me to show growth. This was most disappointing and became a turning point in my career. I had never experienced such disgrace, but it proved to actually be a promotion of my leadership characteristics in the launching of my "next bold move." My misfortune became the gateway for my breakthrough.

I asked myself if I still found joy in my job. Although saddened, I was still interested in my position and performing it at even greater levels. Since Wednesday of the previous week and all weekend long, I had this question on my mind. Finally, Monday morning came and my director and I met, per my request. We had a long meeting, and I was informed of a lot of artificial data and insecurities, but I was more interested in the rightful adjusting of my evaluation. To make a long story short, my evaluation was readjusted with no hesitation as it related to the overall merit award. However, throughout the appraisal the untrue adjustments remained. I didn't press the issue because I didn't think the end result would bring an adequate response. In fact, I was no longer interested in what my director thought of me, and I was successful in receiving the merit raise due to my actions. Galatians 6:10 says, *"For do I now persuade men, or God? or do I seek to please men? for if I yet pleased men, I should not be the servant of Christ"* (Galatians 1:10). I was content that I was doing what was expected of me, and I was *determined*, as long as I was employed, to function enthusiastically and within my capacity. Obviously, I still questioned my confidence in the environment, but my pride wouldn't let me lose the *enthusiasm* I felt toward my players, coworkers, and others that I interacted with on a daily basis. I wasn't going to let the state of affairs steal my joy. I had to forgive but I would not forget. All of this would truly charge my "next bold move!"

For a while, I was reciting, *"Be still, and know that I am God"* (Psalms 46:10). Then God changed gears saying, "Come on up higher!" Although shattered, God blessed me by restoring my broken pieces and giving me a passion that would ultimately motivate me to fulfill my purpose in life. He gave me *"beauty for ashes, the oil of joy for mourning, the garment of praise for the spirit of heaviness..."* (Isaiah 61:3). I was called to transition. My character and my actions led to a more prosperous life. He was taking me out of darkness and into His marvelous light. When I didn't want to jump out of bed because I didn't feel as if I would accomplish anything, I then started to stay up late and rose early, excited about the possibilities and the potential ahead. I was thirsty for God's presence and hungry for His Word and His will for my life. I was certainly going in the right direction because the passion returned; I came alive again. I was ready to continue on the path that God set before me, regardless of the circumstances. Who was I to think that my life would be void of trouble? Jesus, Himself, did no wrong, but endured abysmal persecution during the course of His adult life. As a result of His suffering, the world now has a Savior, one who provides more abundant life on earth and eternal life in heaven to those who receive Him. I sought God's kingdom and His righteousness (See Matthew 6:33). By doing this, I was guaranteed to receive the blessings that God wanted to add to my life. I did not have to worry or become frustrated in the process, for God was with me and He promised to never leave me (See Hebrews 13:5). You must know that by His Word and His Spirit, God leads us in the way that we should go. Who is leading you?

CHAPTER 9

CHARACTER & ACTIONS LEAD TO LIFE

One thing that I like to stress to people that I speak with is that we are "called," and you know that when you are "called" you should answer that C.A.L.L. The way you respond to this C.A.L.L is based on your *character* and *actions* that *lead* to the outcome of your *life*. The Word tells us to make every effort to confirm our calling, and it goes on to state that if we do these things, we will never stumble (See 2 Peter 1:10). At this period in my life, I was certainly ready and willing to do whatever God said to do because I felt so disgruntled. I was ready to disengage myself from the past and prepare for the present and the future. Finally, I surrendered; I let go and let God work.

Although I enjoy sports and athletics, I was not getting the same joy that I used to from them. I functioned as a sports consultant and administrator, and I served as a mentor and liaison for youth across the country. I built them up, encouraged them, and helped them make decisions that would manifest access. But I wasn't able to indisputably do what I was gifted to do because of all the concerns around me. My character and desire was to help others accomplish something; I didn't want to be in the midst of excuses that resulted in nothing. I've always said that God gives me opportunities, and I walk in them – and I won't walk out of them until the time is right. I believe that my steadfast attitude has gotten me a long way. I was feeling a challenge and my character was tested. I asked God to direct my footsteps according to His Word; I knew that my actions had to also follow Him.

One day, I came face-to-face with my need to change my situation, and my character and my actions were significant in allowing this transition in my life. During a Sunday service at church, a preacher spoke regarding "your next bold move." It was so profound that it helped bring my life to its current circumstance. With the guidance of the Holy Spirit, God's protection, and Christ's power, I had nothing to fear because the Bible says, *"The wicked flee when no man pursueth: but the righteous are bold as a lion."* (Proverbs 28:1).

Divine courage and inspiration surged through me and I immediately was given a vision of what I should do to be most effective in the Kingdom. I was already doing it! I just needed to build my legacy by taking the barriers in my life away and feeding my purpose.

Instantly, I thought of going into business for myself. Everyone knows there is a difference between working in an organization and being the chief executive officer. I would make calls, I would operate with integrity, and I would build lives up - not break them down. I would step up to the position God had called me to and carry out my work according to His instructions, *"Withhold not good from them to whom it is due, when it is in the power of thine hand to do it"* (Proverbs 3:27). I was once told that you will never get rich working for someone else. I envisioned launching a program that would change the world. TJ Sports Complete, Inc. would birth from the (H.U.R.T.), which would be healing, presenting a sense of urgency in order to make a lifetime dream a reality by becoming a testimony! My character and my actions led to a new gratification in life, and this would eventually lead others to build their lives stronger too. I remembered the scripture, *"The Lord shall increase you more and more, you and your children"* (Psalms 115:14).

The Lord says, *"My sheep hear my voice, and I know them, and they follow me"* (John 10:27). So, you have to know how God speaks to you. He also says *"Call to me and I will answer you, and I will tell you great and mighty things, which you do not know"* (Jeremiah 33:3). But above all, you must listen and follow Him. We deceive ourselves if we will only hear, rather than also being doers of the Word of God (See James 1:22). I knew He was speaking to me like never before, because He gave me the inspiration, insight, grace, and the motivation to move forward very suddenly. When it is God, you will be driven by God to do it. In just a month's time, the business was incorporated, a layout of the consultation of TJ Speaks Life was established, my client database was formed, and programs to be offered were envisioned: TJ Speaks Life, TJ Sports Camps, TJ Sports Travel, TJ Sports Pages, TJ Sports Apparel, and TJ Sports Grill. I had a company logo, website presence, email address, marketing team, and clients booked for the upcoming year. Before the end of the year, I would be managing a full operation. It was nothing new; I was doing what I have always been doing in sports and athletics all of my years. It was my purpose in life, where I found myself most effective building the Kingdom. I moved from a sideline expert to enhancing my identity and self-worth. I knew I would have to read more books, articles, pamphlets, and listen to more tapes and lectures, but most importantly, I would need to passionately plunge into the Word of God.

I have learned that God does not always call the qualified, but He always qualifies the called! *"Moreover whom he did predestinate, them he also called: and whom he called, them he also justified: and whom he justified, them he also glorified"* (Romans

8:30). Too often, we end up dejected and defeated because we feel inadequate. We feel that we do not have what it takes to be in a certain role or position because we are constantly comparing ourselves. Even when we step up and move into our purpose, we may get plagued with "Imposter Syndrome." We feel like frauds, as though we do not deserve our accomplishments, but that is the lie of the enemy. We must celebrate our achievements, believing that they are evidence of God's blessings and the works of our hands as we exercise the gifts, skills, and talents He has given us.

I had to consider my past, present, and future. I had to come to the conclusion that my past was a learning experience directed by God, my present was a God move because I was confident that I was going in the right direction, and my future is in God's hands. I was certain that I did not want to stay in my present position and present a fake version of myself to others, as if I was alright while growing more and more disenchanted. Whenever you are presented with a God given opportunity, there will be opposition. I wanted to help others succeed and work directly with people who needed my expertise more than I was concerned about my rivals in the workplace. I know that there is nothing too hard for God to get me through. I wanted people to say, "God, through Tamica, I realized my potential, and that is why I am where I am in life today." I want the reputation that causes people to say, "When I could not find my way, God sent Tamica to guide and position me into my next bold move in life." Don't misunderstand me, I did not want to steal God's glory, no. This was not about selfish pride; it was about showing others how God can use people. It doesn't matter if you're at the top of your game or if you've hit rock bottom, God can still use you to bless others and bring them into His Kingdom. I wanted to be in good standing with those around me because I knew I was a servant of Christ, an ambassador of God, and that a good name is more desirable than great riches (See Proverbs 22:1). We must not forget to conduct ourselves in an honorable,

Christ-like way so that others may see our good deeds and glorify God (See 1 Peter 2:12). Also, it is written, "Let the one who boasts boast in the Lord" (1 Corinthians 1:31). More than getting a steady paycheck, I'd rather know that because of my influence, youngsters made their dreams a reality. Ultimately, I want my accomplishments to show in the lives, attitudes, and victorious actions of those who hire me. I was no longer stuck between where I was and where I wanted to be. I knew I was making a decision that I could take pleasure in for the rest of my life.

CHAPTER 10

LIVING, LEARNING & LOVING LIFE

I truly know that success has come my way early in life because I am living, learning, and loving life. I realized that the value of living is to learn. I am not burdened by the cares of this world or the pressure to live up to other people's lofty standards. And as a leader, I have learned that I do not have to be the source of all wisdom; I simply need to recognize good ideas and encourage them. I have settled in my role as a servant of God. This concept has driven me more and more towards professional development in every area of life. I have applied, been accepted into, and attended all sorts of associations to meticulously enhance my proficiency in athletic administration. The Conference office and NCAA staffs have been significant in my growth and notable in their commitment to developing leaders. Resources such as the National Advancement of Collegiate Women in Athletic Administration Institute, the Leadership Institute for Minority Women in Athletics, The Division II Leadership Academy, and the Champs/Life Skills Orientation and Continuing

Education have truly been influential in my advancement.

As a result of all the curriculum studied and ideas shared, I will fashion a generation of "playmakers." These "playmakers" will consist of youth, parents, coaches, administrators, and others interested in the success of those who are making critical transitions in life. TJ Sports Complete, Inc. will provide total support to their needs as they relate to academic and athletic life transitions. I know the importance of being balanced because, "Talent can take you far, but education and the right information can take you even further in life." I want to be a servant to our youth, young adults, parents, and the administrators who lead them. I want to be that point of access to the education and right information for those who would otherwise be uninformed, underserved, ill-advised, and even those who are prepared but are not following the most favorable path. I would hope that through my experiences outlined in this book, people will realize that although obstacles come, you still must make C.H.O.I.C.E.S. that will lead to good success.

When making choices, remember that *change* is not always bad, so be optimistic, always focusing towards the good in the change. Consider the act of changing an opportunity to turn your current situation into something new and better for you. When making choices, we must acknowledge that we need *help*. As I matured in life, I realized more that I needed help to make a good decision. I always involve my family, whether it was a mom and dad situation or a sister and brother in the conversation. The Bible says, *"Plans fail for lack of counsel, but with many advisers they succeed"* (Proverbs 15:22). Don't be afraid to ask for help. You're not in this alone, and so many others have experienced the same challenges as you. It is really tough to try to deal with life without any help. Remember, there is nothing new under the sun. Even if you do not act on their advice, at least you become more equipped and have more *options* to make sound decisions. Above all,

"Trust in the Lord with all thine heart; and lean not unto thine own understanding. In all thy ways acknowledge him, and he shall direct thy paths" (Proverbs 3:5-6). As we make choices, we automatically create options that we must weigh. Anytime you have options, you are in a good situation – whether it looks like it or not. Options allow flexibility, which I learned through my own personal experiences. If you are not flexible and able to bend, you will break.

Our choices fashion our *identity,* which generally becomes a part of a habitual routine of who we are. When making our choices, we must be *committed* to the choice and be confident that it is the best selection. We will have to act upon it and feed it to be successful. The feeding stage is where we will put a lot of *energy* that is necessary for it to be fruitful. Likewise, in many transitions, we feel we are in a difficult position because it causes us to pull from our past and push towards an uncertain future.

Just think, if you hold onto yesterday you will never experience the treasures life has stored up for your future. However, exercising our choices gives us *strength* to make our "next bold move" in life. Choices are perpetual, so you have to gain confidence that you can make good decisions and that they will produce a favorable outcome. Remember, every pull from the past and every push towards the future puts you closer to your destiny. Know that C.H.O.I.C.E.S. are opportunities to succeed, a chance for God to show off His good works in you! Each opportunity we are given in His design is to bring us closer to our purpose and our destiny, with the ultimate goal being that whatever we accomplish brings glory to God.

To all who read *A Ball and a Dream*, God bless you in your future success as you make your "next bold move." In addition, I pray that you allow God to lead you, and that *"the eyes of your heart may be enlightened in order that you may know the hope to which he has called you"* (Ephesians 1:18). For those you know who have not had the opportunity to read this book, I pray you will make the investment in their lives to share this testimony that will encourage them to dream, because, as you and I have learned, dreams do come true.

ABOUT THE AUTHOR

Tamica Smith Jones was named UC Riverside's director of intercollegiate athletics in June of 2015 following two years as the senior associate athletics director for internal affairs and senior woman administrator (SWA) at UT San Antonio. In May of 2016, she was appointed to the NCAA Division I Women's Basketball Championship Sport Committee which, among other things, determines the host institutions and the site of the championship(s) in collaboration with the Women's Basketball Oversight Committee, and selects, seeds and brackets the NCAA Championship.

Smith Jones' primary roles and responsibilities at UTSA included oversight and supervision of women's basketball, volleyball, soccer, softball, cross country, track & field, golf and co-ed cheer, as well as Title IX/gender equity, diversity and inclusion, student-athlete well-being, life skills, community engagement and coaches development. She also served as athletics liaison to the UTSA Student Affairs division and provided strategic planning and assessment.

Smith Jones came to UTSA from Clark Atlanta University, where she led the athletics department beginning in 2008. She was appointed liaison to the office of the president in January 2008 then was promoted to interim director of athletics in December of that year before being named director of athletics in January 2010. Under her leadership, the Panthers captured seven Southern Intercollegiate Athletic Conference (SIAC) Championships, including the first men's basketball title in 46 years and the first-ever women's cross country and volleyball crowns.

Smith Jones also played a vital role in securing funding for numerous projects on campus, including new field turf for the football stadium, a pair of weight room upgrades and a football facility renovation. She established Clark Atlanta's Athletics annual giving fund in 2008, and instituted several new opportunities for student-athlete participation and staff development.

Smith Jones was featured in the Diverse Issues in Higher Ed Magazine in March 2013 for bringing heightened attention toward student-athlete well being and establishing a successful academic support program at Clark Atlanta. Her initiatives included "Grades First Software," which helped to enhance the student-athlete experience and academic success.

The Atlanta, Georgia native is an active member of many professional organizations and committees. She is or has been a member of the National Association of Collegiate Directors of Athletics (featured article on "Balancing your personal and professional brand" in June 2014 NACDA Magazine), Minority Opportunities Athletic Association, National Association of Collegiate Women Athletics Administrators (currently serves as a member of NACWAA Advancement Fund

Committee), NCAA Leadership Selection Committee for Ethnic Males and Females, and Achieving Coaches Excellence Program Selection Committee. Smith-Jones also has served at or presented to the NCAA Committee for Women's Athletics, NCAA Division II Athletic Directors Committee, NCAA Football Coaches Academy and Selection Committee, NCAA CHAMPS/Life Skills Continuing Education Conference, Career in Sports Forum and NCAA Division II Leadership Action Academy.

Before moving into her role as Clark Atlanta's director of athletics, Smith Jones served as the Panthers' director of compliance and SWA for three years. Prior to entering athletics administration, Smith Jones was the head volleyball coach at Clark Atlanta during the 2003-05 seasons. She guided the Panthers to 57 victories in her three years, including four against NCAA Division I teams. Smith Jones led the Clark Atlanta to a 27-11 record in her second campaign and was named SIAC

Coach of the Year, and she followed that with a 21-7 mark in 2005.

Prior to her time at Clark Atlanta, Smith Jones spent four years in various roles at Morris Brown College, also in Atlanta. She was the senior associate athletics director, SWA and head volleyball coach from 1999-2003 in addition to serving as an assistant women's basketball coach in 1999-2000.

Smith Jones was an assistant women's basketball coach at Savannah State in 1997- 98 and then was interim head volleyball and women's basketball coach in 1998-99. She played basketball at Troy (1993-95) and Alabama A&M (1995-97) and also was a member of the Alabama A&M cross country team in 1997.

Smith Jones earned her Bachelor's Degree in Management from Alabama A&M in December 1997, her Master's in Public Administration from Savannah State in December 1999 and completed a certificate program in business administration from Warren National (formerly Kennedy-Western) in February 2005.

To invite Tamica Smith Jones to appear or speak at an event, contact her at:

Tamica Smith Jones, PhD

Email
TJSportsCompleteBookings@gmail.com

Linkedin
https://www.linkedin.com/in/tamica-smith-jones-90094433/

Google Voice Assistant
(404) 939-5336

www.ingramcontent.com/pod-product-compliance
Lightning Source LLC
LaVergne TN
LVHW091153080426
835509LV00006B/666